# OWN YOUR WEEKEND

# OWN YOUR WEEKEND

## A 48-Hour Plan to Live with Intention, Recharge Your Energy, & Declutter Your Mind

with microhabits

Tila Kay, PhD

Copyright © 2025 Box & Bloom
All rights reserved.

No part of this book may be reproduced, or stored in a retrieval system, or transmitted in any form or by any means, electronic, mechanical, photocopying, recording, or otherwise, without express written permission of the publisher.

Under no circumstances shall the publisher, author, or anyone else be held liable for any direct or indirect losses resulting from the use of the information contained within, including, but not limited to, errors, omissions, or inaccuracies. The author is not responsible for any blame, legal liability, damages, reparation, or monetary loss arising from the information in this book, either directly or indirectly.

Legal Notice: This book is protected by copyright and is intended for personal use only. Any alteration, distribution, sale, use, quotation, or paraphrasing of any part or content within this book requires the consent of the author or publisher.

Disclaimer Notice: The information in this document is provided for educational and entertainment purposes only. Every effort has been made to present accurate, up-to-date, reliable, and complete information, but no warranties of any kind are declared or implied. Readers should be aware that the author is not providing legal, financial, medical, or professional advice. By reading this document, the reader agrees that the author is not responsible under any circumstances.

Paperback ISBN 978-1-0697974-0-7
Hardcover ISBN 978-1-0697974-1-4
First Edition
Burnaby, BC, Canada
Cover design by: Box & Bloom
For more books by this author, please visit:
https://boxandbloom.net
For questions, suggestions, or bulk orders, please send an email to contact@boxandbloom.net

 Box & Bloom

# Dedication

*To my husband and my little ray of sunshine. May you always light up my life (and weekends) with joy and powerful happy moments to remember forever.*

## Weekend

(noun.)

*The two day period when you contemplate doing all the things you said you would during the week but end up binge-watching your favorite shows.*

- UNKNOWN

# Table of Contents

Introduction ........................................................... 1
    Why Two Days Can Transform Seven ............. 3
    My Story ............................................................. 4

**Chapter 1 - Closing the Week** ....................................... **7**
    My "Friday Night Lights Off" Ritual ............... 9

**Chapter 2 - The Brain Dump** ......................................... **12**
    The Magic of Emptying Out ........................ 15

**Chapter 3 - Saturday Morning** ...................................... **17**
    Building Your Morning Reset ....................... 19

**Chapter 4 - Fresh Surroundings** ................................... **22**
    Out and About ............................................. 25

**Chapter 5 - Body Tune-Up** ........................................... **28**
    Nourishment and Hydration ....................... 30
    Rest and Recovery ...................................... 32

**Chapter 6 - Inner Glow** ................................................. **34**
    Balance is Key ............................................. 37

**Chapter 7 - Sunday Morning** ........................................ **39**
    The Three-Part Plan .................................... 40
        1. Reflect ................................................ 40
        2. Prioritize ............................................. 41
        3. Organize ............................................. 42
    Can You Look Forward to Monday? ............. 44

**Chapter 8 - Food for Thought.. Literally** ...................... **46**
    The 90-Minute Prep Plan ............................ 48
    Meal Prep Examples ................................... 50
    Avoiding Meal Prep Burnout ...................... 51

    If Meal Prep Isn't Your Thing......................53
**Chapter 9 - Digital Declutter..........................................55**
    Tech Sweep................................................... 56
**Chapter 10 - Financial Refreshment..........................60**
    The Sunday Money Check-In....................... 61
**Chapter 11 - Connection & Relationships..................65**
    Connection for Working Parents.................. 67
**Chapter 12 - Quiet & Creativity....................................71**
    Creative Expression...................................... 73
    Quiet & Creativity for Families.................... 74
    Tips to Protect Quiet & Creative Time...........75
**Your 48-Hour Plan............................................... 77**
    Tips for Long-Term Success......................... 77
    Friday Evening............................................. 78
    Saturday....................................................... 78
    Sunday..........................................................79
    Further Microhabits..................................... 81
**Conclusion............................................................83**
    Resetting Beyond the Weekend.................... 84
**References........................................................... 87**
**About the Author................................................89**

# Introduction

Many of us "live for weekends" and feel really happy that they're here. The reality is, the weekend comes, you sleep in, you might catch up with family, then before you know it, Sunday night comes and you feel dreadful that Monday is so close. My weekends sounded similar to that. I often felt like my weeks ran me instead of the other way around. Monday mornings came too quickly, Tuesdays were spent catching up, and by Thursday, I was already behind again. Maybe you know the feeling: constant low-level energy and feeling never fully caught up or rested. Everything shifted when I began treating the weekend as more than a break. I started seeing it as a container for renewal. Two days, when used with intention, became enough to reset my space, my body, my priorities, and my outlook.

"Owning your weekend" doesn't begin with huge changes. It begins with the smallest possible steps. Such little actions, called **microhabits**, anchor your attempts to have a more rejuvenating weekend in reality.

Researchers studying habit formation have found that it's not willpower that shapes lasting change, but small, repeatable behaviors do [1]. In fact, the more engaging those little actions are to you, the more dopamine is released and you get a sense of reward, making you want to do more of the actions that make you feel happy (see Figure 1). Therefore, habit formation occurs over time. Think of microhabits like seeds. You water them over time, and they grow into stability and shape your identity. Microhabits can look like:

- Drinking one glass of water before coffee.
- Writing down one word to describe your day.
- Stepping outside for two minutes of sunlight.

Stacked together, microhabits create a foundation that makes the strategy of owning your weekend sustainable. You don't need to overhaul your entire weekend. You only need to commit to a few tiny actions, repeated consistently. I will guide you through these habits step by step.

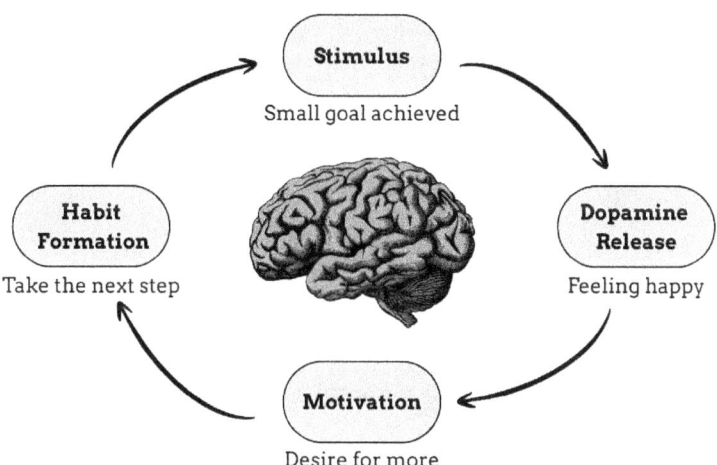

**Figure 1:** Habit formation occurs simultaneously with dopamine release as you practice actions or achieve goals that make you happy.

## Why Two Days Can Transform Seven

This book sheds light on the possibility of transforming your entire week by investing in your weekend. I'm not here to tell you to do more or ruin your hard-earned weekend. I'm here to show you that mindful planning and being present in these two days can be your start to a relaxed, organized week. In a nutshell, owning your weekend, or by what I also call here the weekend reset, is where:

- Friday night becomes the closing exhale.
- Saturday becomes a space to refresh your body and home.

- Sunday becomes the moment to align your mind and priorities for the week ahead.

Microhabits act as anchors. They keep the weekend reset light and doable, even if life gets messy. As you read through this book, you will find **"microhabit nudges"** here and there as reminders to take a moment for yourself throughout your mindful weekend. You do not have to do all of them. Choose the ones that work for you, or use them as insights to create your own microhabits that you feel could commit to in the long run.

## My Story

I completed my PhD in 2024 then gave birth one month right after my defense. As you can imagine, everything was a race. My life was composed of a never-ending cycle of tasks, meetings, deadlines, feeding the baby, learning every detail of how to nurture a child (since I have no family members living in the same country), and lots of Googling. My only breathing room was the weekend when my husband would be off from work and could take care of our child. However, when a new week begins, I feel as compressed and anxious as ever, since I didn't fully rest during the weekend. I'm sure many of you will resonate with me.

As my child completed their first year of life, I started further spiraling into a whirlwind of tasks. Everyone wanted a piece of me, and I was losing myself. I did not pursue any passion, watch a movie, do a hobby, or take some time to do something genuinely for *me*. I started feeling drained, just waiting for the weekend to arrive to take a breath. Something *had* to change. One Friday evening after an exhausting week, I closed my laptop and wrote down three nagging thoughts on a scrap of paper, then tucked it away. This was a transforming revelation. The next morning, I felt lighter. Within weeks of doing this repeatedly, I started feeling more refreshed and at peace with myself the more I did this.

This is what I want for you: not a rigid checklist or me ruining your only restful two days, but a flexible ritual that you can return to **every weekend**. Think of it as a cycle of renewal, powered by habits so small that you can't fail to keep them.

**Let's reflect:** *Think back to last weekend. If you could have added one tiny habit (something that takes less than two minutes) what would it have been?*

Before you move into Chapter One, try this: **write down one word to describe your past week.** This single word becomes your marker, your signal that you are transitioning into reset mode.

Chapter 1

# Closing the Week

There's a quiet power in endings. We often think about how to begin well (think Monday mornings, New Year's resolutions, fresh notebooks, etc.), but how often do we pause to notice how we finish? The way you close your week sets the tone for how you enter your weekend, and ultimately how you begin the next week.

My Friday evenings often looked like a blur. I would half-finish emails, rush through dinner, and collapse on the couch with my laptop still pinging nearby. The week didn't feel "done." It just spilled into Saturday, and by Sunday I was already worried about Monday. There was no boundary.

What I needed was closure. A ritual that told my mind and body, "The week is complete. You can truly rest now." That is what this chapter is about: creating a finish line so you can step fully into your weekend reset.

Psychologists call closure the **Zeigarnik effect** [2]. Our brains cling to unfinished tasks. That's why you find yourself thinking about that one email you didn't send or the conversation you avoided. Unless you create a clear stopping point, your mind keeps spinning. A closing ritual does two things:

1. Signals to your brain that the week is over.
2. Gives you permission to rest without guilt.

The closing ritual doesn't have to be long. In fact, the shorter and more consistent it is, the better.

## My "Friday Night Lights Off" Ritual

Every Friday before I step away from work, I *shut down* my laptop, put my phone on silent, and literally turn off the lamp on my desk. That simple act of flicking a switch tells me: *You've done enough. The week is over.* The first time I tried it, I laughed at how silly it seemed. Now, every Friday, that lamp turning off feels like a burden is off my shoulders.

---

**Microhabit Nudge:** *Try creating your own signal of closure. It could be:*

- *Shutting your laptop and placing it neatly on the side of your desk.*
- *Putting your work bag in a closet.*
- *Lighting a candle as a "week is done" ritual.*

*Keep it simple, repeatable, and **sensory**.*

---

Of course, it's not just physical space that needs closing; it's mental space, too. I began practicing what I now call the "Friday Sweep." I spend ten minutes doing a quick check:

- Write down lingering tasks that didn't get finished.
- Note any important reminders for Monday.
- Capture stray ideas in a journal or notes app.

This tiny act stops my brain from buzzing. I don't need to carry the weight of "don't forget this" all weekend. It's already written down and waiting for me when I return.

---

**Microhabit Nudge:** *End your workweek with a two-minute list. Write down three things:*

1. *What you completed this week.*
2. *What you'll start with on Monday.*
3. *One thing you're letting go of.*

---

Closing the week isn't about cramming in just one more email or rushing through a to-do list. It's about creating a ritual of transition. When you close the week with intention, you're doing more than finishing tasks. You're protecting your energy. You're teaching yourself that rest is part of productivity. So tonight, when Friday arrives, ask yourself: *How do I want to mark this ending?*

---

**Microhabit Nudge:** *Before leaving your workspace on Friday, take a slow breath and say out loud: The week is finished. I will return on Monday.*

---

The closing ritual is the first step of your 48-hour reset plan. When you close your week with a mindful action, you create a clear boundary that allows everything else (rest, reflection, and planning) to flow smoothly. It doesn't even have to look the same every week. What matters is the signal you give yourself: *I am done for now. I can rest.*

Chapter 2

# The Brain Dump

Have you ever noticed how loud your mind gets the moment you try to relax? You sit down to read or watch something, and suddenly your brain pipes up: "Don't forget to pay that bill. Did you ever reply to that email? Oh, and next week's meeting...". It's like the volume knob on your thoughts has been turned all the way up. That's because your mind hates carrying unfinished business. It will keep reminding you, over and over, until you succumb and actually do that task, even though you don't want to.

This is why the **brain dump** is such a crucial part of owning your weekend. It's one of the most freeing things you can do on a Friday night. Think of a brain dump as housekeeping for your mind. Just like you wouldn't want to cook dinner in a messy kitchen, you don't want to enter your weekend with a cluttered head. A brain dump is simply writing down everything swirling in your mind: tasks, worries, ideas, or random thoughts. The goal is to *release*.

---

**Microhabit Nudge:** *Keep a dedicated notebook (or a notes app) only for your brain dumps. Use the same spot to write every time. Over weeks, this becomes your* **mental dropbox**.

---

The beauty of a brain dump is its flexibility. You can spend 20 minutes or just three. A brain dump can look like this:

1. Grab a paper or open a blank notebook.

2. Set a timer for 2–5 minutes (or as long as you like).
3. Write whatever pops into your mind. Big, small, silly, important. Everything goes down.
4. Stop when the timer ends.

Sometimes, my page looks like this:

- Finish laundry
- Call Mom
- That weird idea about starting a garden
- Did I pay the credit card?
- Outline presentation for Tuesday
- Buy new running shoes

---

**Microhabit Nudges:**

- *Use categories if your mind feels scattered. Try headings like "Work," "Home," "Health," "Random." It helps group thoughts so they feel less overwhelming.*
- *Before you close your notebook, put a star next to just one thing you'll handle next week.*

## The Magic of Emptying Out

The first time I did this, I was shocked at how much noise came out. I didn't realize I was holding on to so many scraps of mental clutter. When it was on paper, it no longer owned my attention. This is the hidden power of a brain dump: it shifts worries from "I have to remember this" to "this is safely captured." That single shift reduces stress and opens mental space for right-now presence.

Your weekend is not the time to solve everything., but it *is* the time to give your mind permission to rest. So tonight, take a few minutes to empty your mind onto a piece of paper. See what shows up!

As you move through the subsequent chapters, it might be a good idea to take notes in your journal/notebook. I have included here a sample page of how you can organize your notes as you read:

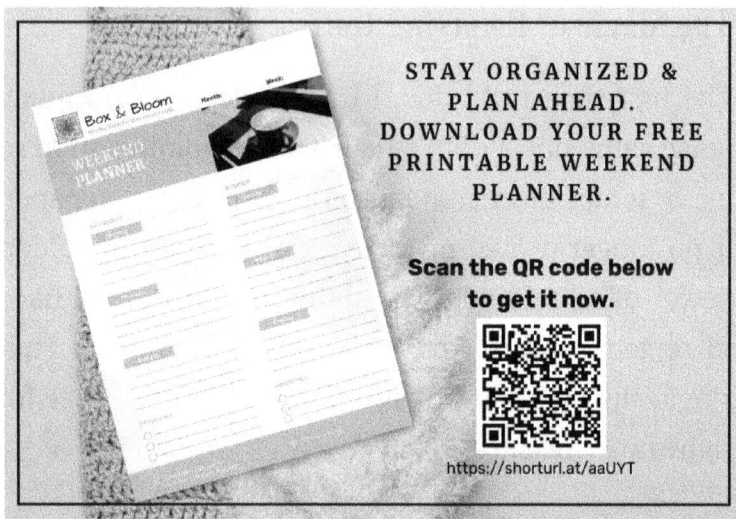

Chapter 3

# Saturday Morning

The way you step into the first hours of Saturday morning shapes everything that follows. If you roll out of bed, grab your phone, and get swept straight into notifications, you'll carry that scattered energy all weekend. On the other hand, if you choose something different, something slower and more intentional, you can set a tone of serenity and focus that lasts until Sunday night.

I used to treat Saturday mornings like recovery missions: sleep in, scroll aimlessly, half-eat breakfast while doing chores. By noon, I already felt behind. The weekend which was supposed to refresh me started with me chasing it instead. That's when I decided to reframe Saturday mornings. I began treating them as a kind of gentle launch. Not an overly scheduled morning but a steady, grounding, and repeated experience.

\*\*\*\*

**Anchors** are small recurring habits that stabilize our lives and give consistent signals to your brain and body that you are in reset mode now [3]. Saturday morning can be one of those anchors. If you start with something that feels swift, you'll notice:

- Your mind slows down.
- Your body relaxes.
- You feel less rushed.

---

**Microhabit Nudge:** *Resist the urge to pick up your phone for the first 20 minutes of your Saturday.*

---

## Building Your Morning Reset

My Saturday morning looks like:

- I make a warm drink (sometimes coffee, sometimes tea, sometimes cinnamon).
- I make a healthy, protein-rich breakfast.
- I sit by the window.
- I let my child share the plate with me.
- I let myself be quiet for a few minutes if possible, usually with a notebook nearby.
- Sometimes I write a few lines, other times I just breathe.

You don't need to copy my routine. Design your own routine to fit your lifestyle and preferences. Ask yourself: *What makes me feel calm and clear?* Maybe it's movement, maybe it's quiet, maybe it's a mix. Try building your morning ritual from these three categories:

1. **Stillness**: Journaling, meditation, or slow breathing.
2. **Movement**: A short walk, light stretching, or dancing in your kitchen.
3. **Nourishment**: A mindful breakfast, a warm drink, or just a tall glass of water.

Pick one or more of these. Your morning routine can take 15 minutes or an hour. It's up to you.

---

**Microhabit Nudge:** *Pair your morning drink with one page of reflection. Answer a simple question like, "How do I want to feel this weekend?"*

---

If you like stretching in the morning, the below figure includes some suggested poses to incorporate in your daily routine.

**Figure 2:** Suggested stretching poses to implement on your Saturday morning.

Your morning reset becomes muscle memory the more you practice it. Just like brushing your teeth signals bedtime, your Saturday morning ritual signals peace. This signal makes everything else flow more easily: cleaning your home, cooking, connecting with others, and planning your week.

**Microhabit Nudge:** *If you struggle to stick with it, set out a tiny cue the night before. Lay out your journal and pen. Prep the coffee pot. Place your yoga mat in the corner. Make it easy to begin.*

Imagine your next Saturday morning. Instead of rushing, what if you gave yourself a 20-minute pause to do your thing? This small act can help you claim your weekend. Try it.

Chapter 4

# Fresh Surroundings

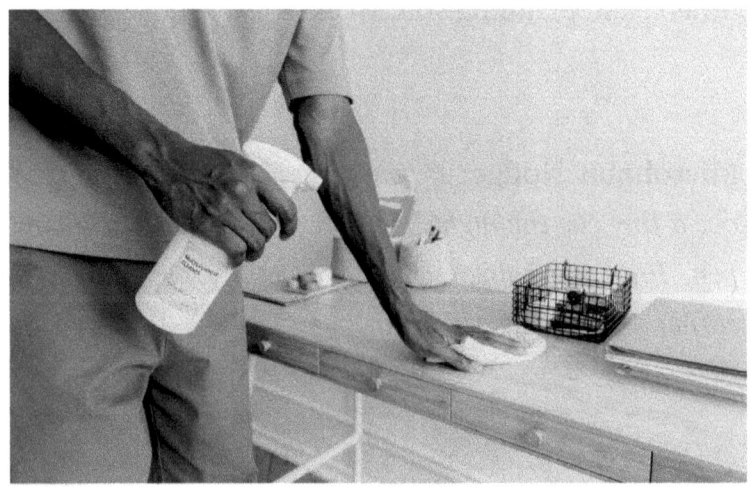

There's a deep relief that comes when you look around your home and realize it doesn't weigh on you. No piles screaming for attention. No clutter in the corners pulling at your focus. A clear space is a clear mind. In fact, it has been shown that the environment around you influences how your mind thinks and functions [4]. This chapter is about creating mental clarity without spending the whole day scrubbing and cleaning.

I used to avoid the urge to not clean everything during the weekend. My Saturdays were often swallowed by chores that felt endless: laundry, dishes, vacuuming, you name it. I would start one thing and get distracted by another. By evening, I was tired, and cranky, not to mention that I didn't actually rest as I'm supposed to in order to reenergize for the demanding week ahead. It took me a long time to realize the key wasn't to do everything. It was just to do enough to organize my home's atmosphere and feel more peace.

Research has shown that clutter increases stress, decreases focus, and even makes it harder to make decisions [5, 6]. When your environment is noisy, your brain feels noisy. Take a look at Figure 3 which shows how cluttered homes were associated with higher cortisol levels and increasing depressed mood throughout the day, especially in women [7]. On the other hand, a **15-minute tidy-up** can lower cortisol levels and improve your mood. You can reset your space in under an hour. It doesn't need to look perfect and you don't have to reorganize every drawer or scrub the fridge. Save the deep cleaning for another dedicated time. We're focusing here on developing a schedule for *every* weekend. Your home only needs to feel peaceful enough so that your nervous system relaxes. A few pointers include:

- Clearing the surfaces (kitchen counters, coffee table, nightstand, etc.).
- Emptying or tidying one "stress point" (that corner of paper piles, the laundry mountain, or the messy entryway). Each weekend, choose one stress point to tackle in more depth.
- Resetting the vibe (open a window, light a candle, or put on calming music).

---

**Microhabit Nudge:** *When you walk into a room, put away just one thing that's out of place.*

---

Own Your Weekend

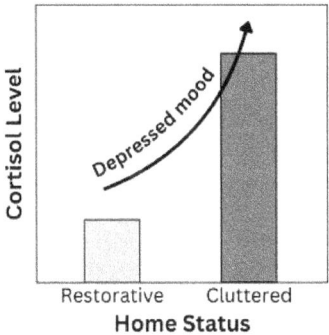

**Figure 3:** Comparison of cortisol levels in clean (restorative) and unorganized (cluttered homes) and the association of a cluttered home status with increasing depressed mood [7].

**Out and About**

Once you've given your home a light reset, **don't stay inside all day.** Go out. Leave your refreshed space and let it wait for you. This is your reward moment! You've taken care of your environment, and now it's time to take care of your spirit. Stepping out for a few hours makes your return home feel more grounding, because your home will greet you with a clean slate.

What counts as an outing? Well, it can be anything that lets you breathe outside of your work routine. For example:

- Coffee or brunch with a friend.
- A long walk in nature.

- Browsing a bookstore or market.
- Visiting family or neighbors.
- Running errands (!), if you do it with presence instead of rushing.

The key is not the activity itself but the shift in energy. You are reminding yourself that life is more than checklists and tasks. You are allowed joy, leisure, and connection.

---

**Microhabit Nudge:** *Before leaving for an outing, set a timer for five minutes and do a quick sweep of shoes, coats, or mail. Returning to a clutter-free entryway makes the reset twice as powerful.*

---

There's something beautiful about coming back to a tidy space after being out in the world. It feels like your home is welcoming you, ready to hold you as you move into the next part of your weekend. This feeling strengthens the habit loop: you start to connect the act of tidying with the reward of peace.

Resetting your space is not about aesthetics or impressing guests. It's about creating an environment where you can think, breathe, and rest without distractions. By the time you finish this step, you've shifted your environment and your energy, and now you're ready to move into caring for your body in the next chapter.

Chapter 5

# Body Tune-Up

After you've refreshed your space and stepped out for a few hours, it's time to shift attention inward to your body. Your environment sets the tone for your thoughts, but your body carries you forward.

For me, this was always the hardest part to honor. I used to fill weekends with chores, social obligations, or endless catch-up tasks. I often didn't know how to decline social gatherings that *I didn't want to be a part of.* This drained me, especially after feeling that my weekend is gone in the pursuit of pleasing others. Movement and rest were squeezed into the margins, if at all. My body felt like the last item on the list, and I started to gain weight. When I flipped the script and placed my body at the center of my priorities, my energy multiplied, my focus sharpened, and I could meet Monday without the dragging weight of exhaustion.

Your body carries stress, fatigue, and mental clutter. When you release that tension physically, your mind follows. Physical activity isn't punishment nor does it require a marathon workout. What your body needs most is **gentle, intentional movement**. Science has shown [8] that regular movement (even just 20 minutes a day) can:

- Lower stress hormones.
- Improve sleep quality.
- Boost mood through endorphins.
- Increase mental clarity and focus.

Engaging in aerobic exercises, or physical movement of any sort for that matter, has been linked to affecting the mood, cognitive function, and central nervous system development [9]. Some ideas you can try to refresh your physical fitness are:

- A walk outside, noticing the world with fresh eyes.
- A yoga or stretch session in your living room.
- Dancing to music in the kitchen.
- A casual bike ride or a brief swim.
- A gym session if that's your happy place.

---

**Microhabit Nudge:** *Whenever you stand up from sitting, stretch your arms overhead and take one deep breath.*

---

### Nourishment and Hydration

Movement is only half the equation. Resetting your body also means giving it fuel. Too often, your work week slides into extremes: skipping meals, overeating takeout, or relying on caffeine to push through chores. A reset weekend invites balance.

- **Drink more water than you think you need.** It has been reported that even mild dehydration (i.e., that causes 1-2% loss in body mass) can result in reduced cognitive function

and having a bad mood, higher fatigue, and lower alertness [10].
- **Eat at least one colorful, nutrient-dense meal.** Different-colored foods, even if apparently the same (like white and purple cauliflower) can have different nutrients. Aiming to include foods from every natural color in your diet is a great way to increase gut microbiome adaptability, improve antioxidant levels, decrease mental health issues, decrease blood pressure issues, and enhance the mood [11]. Ideally, alternate between the different colors of food, try a new food every week, and prepare foods in different ways (like steaming, roasting, or having them raw).

When I started weaving these small shifts into my weekends, I was surprised at how quickly they changed my energy. A big glass of water after my morning walk did more for my clarity than another cup of coffee could. Also, incorporating these habits into my weekends started showing me a relief in my stomach and feeling better in my own body. Increasing physical activity combined with a balanced diet leads to weight loss (or management), which lets you walk with lighter steps. Therefore, I started to consciously plan what to eat and drink during my whole week.

## Rest and Recovery

Rest is often associated with sitting on the couch, binge-watching a show, or sleeping for long stretches in the daylight. However, after those "restful" activities, you often come out heavy-headed and often regret the hours you could have spent on truly rejuvenating actions. The part most of us resist is actual true rest. That might mean:

- A 20-minute power nap.
- Sitting quietly with a favorite drink.
- Watching one episode of something.
- Practicing slow, deep breathing.
- Recognizing what your body is telling you.

---

**Microhabit Nudge:** *Before bed on Saturday, place a glass of water on your nightstand. Drink it first thing on Sunday morning before reaching for your phone.*

---

Resetting your body doesn't mean overhauling your fitness routine. It means honoring the truth that your body deserves. When you move, nourish, and rest, you give back to yourself.

Chapter 6

# Inner Glow

If the body carries our energy and the mind carries our thoughts, the soul carries our meaning. Without tending to your inner self, even the most organized refreshment plan can fall flat. You can have a clean space and an energized body, but if your soul still feels drained, Sunday night arrives and you're left wondering, *What was all that for?*

There was a period when my weekends looked productive on the surface (a tidy home and a stocked fridge), but I still carried an emptiness into the week. It wasn't until I began making space for the things that nourished me deeply, such as spirituality and connection with something beyond my everyday life.

Your soul is the quiet center that keeps you steady in a noisy world. When you take care of it, you reconnect with what truly matters. This doesn't have to be complicated or mystical. It's simply about creating space for the practices, experiences, and moments that remind you of your deeper self. There's no single right way to reset your soul, and that's the beauty of it. This is a personal preference. What nourishes me might not be what nourishes you, but here are some directions to explore:

- **Creativity:** Drawing, writing, cooking, playing an instrument or a game, or any activity where you lose track of time.
- **Spirituality:** Prayer, meditation, reading religious texts, or walking in nature with mindfulness.
- **Reflection:** Journaling about your week, noting what you're grateful for, or writing down lessons you've learned.

- **Connection:** Spending intentional time with people who lift you up, or having a meaningful conversation without distractions.
- **Silence:** Simply sitting in stillness, without reaching for a screen or a task, and letting yourself be.

Did you know that practicing mindful meditation (that is, the training of one's mind to be aware of internal and external experiences at the moment with no judgement) not only reduces stress and anxiety but also has been linked to maintaining body weight after a weight loss journey [12]? Furthermore, religiosity and spirituality have been linked to life longevity and they resemble ways of improving cardiovascular function, personal growth, and sense of purpose [13].

\*\*\*\*

One Saturday, I decided to replace my usual cleaning routine with a 10-minute journaling exercise. I wrote down three questions:

1. What do I need to release myself from this week?
2. What am I carrying forward with gratitude?
3. What do I want to invite in next week?

It felt awkward at first, like I was forcing myself into something artificial. Then, as I kept writing, I noticed that my shoulders dropped and that I had the sense that I wasn't just reacting to life anymore.

**Microhabit Nudges:**

- *Light a candle or incense before beginning any reflective or creative practice. The small ritual signals to your brain: this is sacred time.*
- *Each Saturday night, write down one thing you're grateful for. Place the note in a jar. Over time, you'll build a visible reminder of joy.*
- *Every time you step outside, take one mindful breath and notice one detail of beauty around you. It can be the sky, a leaf, or a stranger's smile.*

## Balance is Key

The temptation here can be overloading your soul with too many practices at once. Resist that. You don't need a full meditation retreat every Saturday evening. You also do not need to do every hobby you have put off for a while. In fact, piling on rituals defeats the purpose. Instead, choose one or two practices that feel alive to you right now. Next weekend, you might choose something different. The soul thrives on variation and freedom.

When you give attention to your soul, your weekend shifts from surface-level productivity to something richer, from doing more to *being* more. You start the week not just prepared, but grounded. You walk into Monday with a sense of wholeness that no one else can give you.

Chapter 7

# Sunday Morning

Sunday morning has a certain energy. The week behind you feels finished, the week ahead feels unwritten. It's a threshold moment, even intimidating to some.

Without a solid plan, weeks tend to run us instead of the other way around. Monday can hit like a wave: meetings scattered across the calendar, grocery lists incomplete, and the sudden realization laundry isn't folded or important messages aren't answered. It left me on the defensive. When I began using Sunday mornings for planning, Monday wasn't a crash landing, but a gentle takeoff. I knew my top priorities, had a handle on our household's meals, and I had already cleared the fog from my mind.

### The Three-Part Plan

Think of your Sunday planning as a three-part ritual: **Reflect, Prioritize, Organize.**

**1. Reflect**

Start with a pause. Before you dive into tasks and lists, look back. Ask yourself:

- What worked well last week?
- What drained me?
- Did I take care of myself?
- Is there anything I need to let go of before starting fresh?

Reflection clears the mental clutter. It also helps you notice patterns. If every Sunday you're writing "I felt exhausted," it's a sign that something deeper needs attention.

**Microhabit Nudge:** *Keep a running list of "lessons learnt" from your reflections. Glance back at it once a month. It's like a private compass guiding you forward.*

## 2. Prioritize

Once you've looked back, shift your gaze forward. This is where many of us get overwhelmed. The list of tasks feels endless. Instead of writing every possible thing, focus on the big rocks. Ask yourself:

- What are the three most important things I want to accomplish this week?
- If everything else falls away, what will make me feel proud by Friday?

**Microhabit Nudge:** *Use a sticky note for your weekly "Top 3." Place it somewhere visible: on your fridge, desk, or inside your planner.*

## 3. Organize

Now you can get practical. This step is about aligning your tasks with real time and space.

- Open your calendar. Fill in appointments, deadlines, or non-negotiables.
- Add in your Top 3 priorities first. Protect time for them as if they were meetings with your future self.
- Block out self-care and rest every day of the week, even if it's just 30 minutes of reading, a walk, or sitting on the balcony.
- Look at your meal prep plans, grocery runs, or errands. Slot them into realistic windows. Outsource help if you can.

This step isn't about cramming everything in. It's about designing your week with **intention**.

---

**Microhabit Nudge:** *Before you close your planner, circle one block of free time and label it "unscheduled." Protect it. This is your personal breathing room.*

---

The gruesome truth is that no plan survives perfectly. Life happens: kids get sick, projects run long, and moods shift. The purpose of planning is not to lock your week into a rigid schedule, but to give your week shape and direction, like a map, so you can bend without breaking when surprises arise.

---

**Microhabit Nudge:** *At the end of each day, quickly review your plan. Adjust tomorrow's tasks instead of carrying guilt about what didn't get done.*

---

If you want to take your planning ritual further, here are a few simple add-ons that can deepen the process:

- **Gratitude list:** Write down 2–3 things from last week you're thankful for.
- **Weekly intention:** Choose one word or phrase to carry into the week. This can be a value, focus, or feeling you want to guide you. (Examples: "steadiness," "kindness," "volunteering," "accomplishment," "clarity.")
- **Family sync:** If you live with others, consider spending ten minutes aligning schedules.

When you finish your planning, close your calendar with something small but intentional. Brew a coffee, light a candle, or play your favorite song.

A Sunday planning ritual gives you confidence and shifts you from being reactive to proactive. When Monday morning comes, you won't need to scramble. You'll already know your plan.

**Can You Look Forward to Monday?**

Most people treat Monday as something to survive, but you can flip that script by giving yourself something to look forward to at the start of the week. Choose a simple but engaging activity you genuinely enjoy and schedule it for Monday evening. This could be a dinner date with a friend, joining a fitness class you love, or setting aside time for a personal hobby. By placing it on your calendar ahead of time, you create a positive anchor that changes how you approach the day. Rather than dreading Monday, you begin anticipating the reward waiting for you after work.

The key is to keep it realistic and energizing, not another obligation that feels heavy. For example, plan a recipe you're excited to try, a short walk in a favorite park, or an episode of a show you've been saving, paired with something cozy like a cup of tea. Think of it as a gift to yourself that transforms Monday from a grind into the gateway of the week. Over time, this habit reframes your mindset: Mondays stop being the "end of freedom" and instead become an intentional space for connection, joy, and small wins.

In fact, I have prepared a great list of activities that you could consider doing on Monday night to get you started. See the image below for details.

Chapter 8

# Food for Thought.. Literally

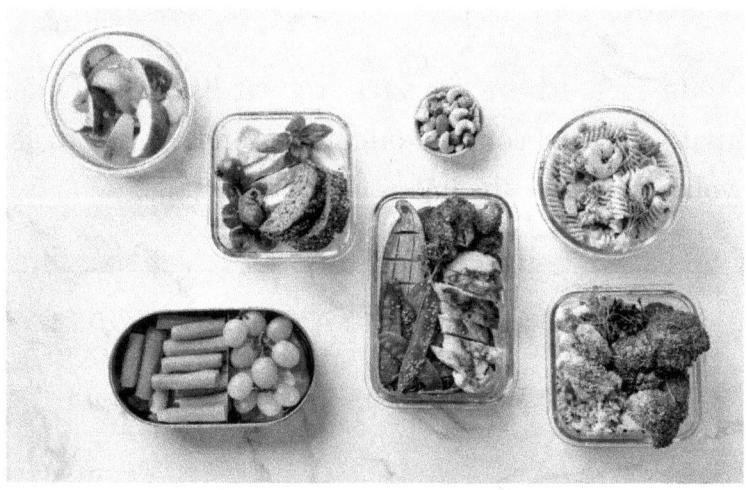

The way you eat across the week shapes your energy, focus, and mood. Yet when life gets busy, meals are often the first thing to slip away. That's why Sunday meal prep is a cornerstone of owning your weekend (and week!). We've all been there: cooking for hours, eating bland containers of the same thing all week, or ordering expensive and unhealthy takeout. When you plan meals that work for you, you reduce decision fatigue, save money, and support your energy.

Decision fatigue is real [14]. It drains energy, causes irritability, mental exhaustion, brain fog, and procrastination. By the time Monday night rolls around, the last thing most of us want to ask is "What should I cook for dinner?" That's when takeout menus and carb-heavy snacks sneak in. Then, you feel awful for consistently eating unhealthy food and already dreading school mornings when you want to prepare lunch boxes for your kids (if applicable) and are just standing in the kitchen browsing the internet for ideas. The frustration multiplies when you don't have all the ingredients for a certain recipe.

Meal prep helps you front-load your choices. You decide once, prepare once, and reap the rewards for days. It's also a way of caring for your future self. When you come home tired, instead of facing an empty fridge, there's a container of soup ready to warm up or pre-chopped vegetables waiting for a quick stir-fry. That moment of relief is gold.

**Microhabit Nudge:** *Think of meal prep not as a chore, but as writing yourself a love letter you'll open midweek.*

Keep meal prep simple by focusing on three categories:

- **Proteins** (chicken, beans, eggs, fish, tofu)
- **Vegetables** (raw for snacks, roasted or sautéed for meals)
- **Carbs and grains** (rice, quinoa, sweet potatoes, whole grain pasta)

Mix and match throughout the week. If you prepare even one item from each category, you already have the building blocks for multiple meals. Aim for one batch of something you can stretch across three meals. It could be soup, a grain salad, or a roasted tray of vegetables.

### The 90-Minute Prep Plan

If you're new to meal prepping, this framework could fit comfortably into a Sunday afternoon:

1. **Make a plan** (10 minutes)

- Jot down three dinners, two lunches, and breakfast ideas. Start from things you know.
- Write a grocery list.
2. **Shop smart** (20 minutes if you're efficient, or longer if it's a big run). Shop online and get it delivered ahead if you prefer.
3. **Batch cook** (60 minutes)
    - Roast two trays of vegetables.
    - Cook or marinate one protein (like chicken or lentils).
    - Prepare a simple carb (like quinoa or brown rice).
    - Chop raw veggies for snacks.

By the end, you'll have at least 4–5 mix-and-match meals plus grab-and-go options.

****

Since we continue to gain insight from those around us through shared experiences, I would like to share with you some hacks I learnt from women I met. A mom of **seven** told me she doesn't even think of what to cook for the coming week. She sticks to certain meals that rotate every six weeks. Another mom shared that her schedule looks like this: Sunday is for pastas, Monday is for a chicken dish with rice, Tuesday is for Chinese food, Wednesday is for Indian dishes, and so on. This decreases the mental fatigue on her and helps her family know what to expect every week.

## Meal Prep Examples

Pick the meal prep "theme" that excites you most this week. You can rotate between them for variety. The below are three weekly prep setups you could try:

### Example 1: The Mediterranean

- Roasted chicken thighs with lemon and garlic
- Couscous with parsley and olive oil
- Chopped cucumber and tomato salad
- Hummus with carrot sticks
- Overnight oats with berries and nuts

### Example 2: The Plant-Based Boost

- Lentil and vegetable stew
- Roasted sweet potatoes
- Quinoa with herbs
- Spinach and chickpea salad jars, with a lemon/citrus dressing on the side
- Chia seed pudding with almond milk and fruit

### Example 3: The Quick Comfort

- Baked salmon with lemon

- Brown rice
- Roasted broccoli and carrots
- Turkey chili (can freeze half)
- Greek yogurt with honey and granola

---

**Microhabit Nudge:** *Write down 3 "emergency meals" you can make in 10 minutes. Stick it inside your pantry door for when energy runs low.*

---

To further support you, I have created a 30-day dinner plan designed to accommodate four people per dinner and most of the recipes can be prepared in one pot. See the image below for more details.

## Avoiding Meal Prep Burnout

One trap is making prep too ambitious. Five new recipes in one Sunday will only leave you exhausted. Instead:

- Stick to familiar recipes you know well.
- Choose 1–2 "anchor meals" you can eat multiple times.
- Allow space for spontaneous dinners. Not every meal needs to be prepped.
- Keep flavor boosters handy (like hot sauce, dressings, and fresh herbs).

---

**Microhabit Nudge:** *Prep less than you think you need. Running out by Friday is better than wasting food you never ate.*

---

Another thing to keep in mind is effort. Consider investing in appliances that decrease the time and physical energy required for cooking (like an airfryer, an electric pressure cooker, etc.). Search methods for decreasing workload, such as using a flat sheet tray in the oven to prepare pancakes instead of flipping them one by one on the stovetop. Subscribe in meal plan boxes or grocery delivery/pick up services; this has gotten us through our first year of parenthood. Lastly, I found that keeping the links of recipes I like saved in a dedicated list on my phone saves me a lot of time to find them again (save yourself moments like: "Oh! I watched it on Instagram but now I don't know where it is!" and "my child really liked that muffin recipe but I can't remember where I got it from"). Save that recipe the moment you realize it is one to keep.

To make meal prep stick, pair it with small habits:

- Wash/store produce immediately after grocery shopping.
- Always have a "default lunch" (like a wrap or salad kit) ready to assemble.
- Keep a list of go-to recipes on your fridge.
- End Sunday prep by packing at least one grab-and-go meal for Monday.

## If Meal Prep Isn't Your Thing

Well, many of us like to have fresh meals cooked on the day of. Even though meal prep can allow for that, some people may just not like doing it. In that case, it would be beneficial to dedicate some time this weekend to plan ahead what you and your family would like to have for breakfast, lunch, dinner, and snacks for the entire week. Then, prepare a list of grocery items missing from your fridge and pantry to make shopping more streamlined with your plans. I have tried this method for many years, and it prevented me from scrambling at the last minute saying things like "Uh-oh, I wish we had more lemons" or "Today has been a long day and I'm not in the mood to think of what to cook for dinner."

When you finish planning and/or cooking this Sunday, pause for a moment. Feel the sense of relief that future you will thank you for. You now have created space for peace of mind, health, and energy.

Chapter 9

# Digital Declutter

Your phone buzzes. Another notification slides across the screen. Without even realizing it, you're pulled in, clicking, scrolling, and consuming. Minutes slip away. Sometimes hours. We live in an always-on world. When unmanaged, technology drains focus, disrupts sleep, and leaves you feeling scattered. Recent research investigated how digital clutter can affect productivity, psychological wellbeing, and digital security, and in some cases, it has been linked to physical hoarding [15, 16].

I used to sleep with my phone next to my pillow. Every morning, the first thing I did was scroll through emails and social media. I thought I was staying on top of things and connecting with far-away family members. In reality, I was draining my energy before the day even began. One weekend, I decided to move my charger across the room. Now, when I wake up, I can stretch or simply breathe before I let the world in.

This chapter is about reclaiming digital control. Think of your digital world as a house. Over time, it collects clutter: unread emails, unused apps, notifications, tabs, photos, messages, etc. Unlike a physical mess, you can't always see it, but you *feel* it:

- The stress of 481 unread emails.
- The ping of group chats that never stops.
- The endless scroll when you only meant to check the weather (then you forget that you wanted to check the weather!).

**Tech Sweep**

Set aside one focused hour in your weekend to do a digital sweep. Consider this roadmap:

1. **Clear the notifications**
    - Turn off non-essential alerts.
    - Leave only calls, texts, and calendar reminders on.
2. **Organize apps**
    - Delete what you don't use.
    - Group essentials into folders.
    - Move distracting apps off your home screen.
3. **Tame email**
    - Unsubscribe from 5–10 newsletters you never read.
    - Archive everything older than a month.
    - Create a "To Reply" folder for important messages.
4. **Photo cleanup**
    - Delete duplicates and blurry shots.
    - Make an album for favorites.
    - Back up to the cloud or an external storage device.
5. **Social media audit**
    - Unfollow accounts that drain you.
    - Mute groups or chats that clutter your time.
    - Set app limits if necessary.

Digital decluttering once is helpful, but **creating boundaries** is the key. You design the rules that protect your attention. Some practical boundaries to consider are:

- **Phone-free mornings**: Don't check your phone for the first 30 or so minutes of the day.
- **Screen-free meals**: No devices at the table.
- **The parking spot**: Keep your phone in a drawer or on a shelf during focus work.
- **Night mode**: Set devices to "Do Not Disturb" two hours before bed.
- **Social media slots**: Decide *when* you check, instead of opening the apps endlessly.

---

**Microhabit Nudge:** *Pick just one boundary this week. Small limits are easier to keep.*

---

Repeatable actions can further create lasting change in your technology use. For example:

- **The 1-tap rule**: If an app takes more than one tap to open, you'll use it less. Move distracting apps off the front page.
- **Delete at least one app every month.** If you haven't used it, you don't need it.

- **Inbox zero ritual**: Archive or delete emails until your inbox is clear, or is at a limit that doesn't intimidate you.
- **Digital sunset**: Turn off Wi-Fi at a set hour each night.

Technology isn't going away. The point isn't to escape it but to design a relationship where *you* are in control. The goal of this step isn't a perfectly clean phone or inbox. It's peace of mind. When you start the coming week, you'll notice differences in your work, restfulness, and relationships.

Chapter 10

# Financial Refreshment

Money is often the quiet stress in our lives. We don't always notice it until we feel the weight: a forgotten bill, a surprise expense, or the realization that we spent more than we intended. Our brains are wired to avoid discomfort. Bills, bank statements, and budgeting feel like tedious chores, so we push them aside. That avoidance can create anxiety that lingers in the background all week. A 20-minute financial reset on Sunday can help:

- lower stress by giving you a clear picture of your money.
- prevent small problems from snowballing into emergencies.
- free mental energy so you can focus on work, family, and resting.

## The Sunday Money Check-In

Consider the below framework for refreshing your relationship with your finances. Aim for a 15–20 minute session each Sunday. It can give you control and reduce financial decision fatigue during the week.

### Step 1: Gather Everything

- Bank statements, credit card info, bills due this week, etc.
- Receipts or notes for any irregular expenses.
- Your paycheck or income information as applicable.

### Step 2: Review & Reflect

- Compare what you spent last week to what you expected.
- Identify any unexpected expenses.

- Celebrate small wins: did you stick to a plan, save a little, or pay down a balance?

---

**Microhabit Nudge:** *Keep a running "Wins" list in your notebook. Noticing progress builds momentum.*

---

### Step 3: Plan the Week

- Pre-authorize any upcoming bills or payments.
- Allocate funds for groceries, gas, and other essentials.
- Decide on one fun spending item (i.e., a small, intentional treat).

Refer to Figure 4 below for a visual representation of the suggested allocation of finances.

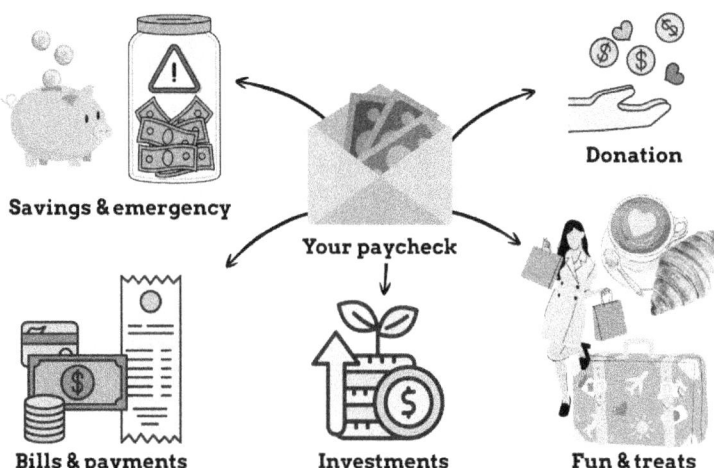

**Figure 4:** Finances flowchart suggestion for when getting your paycheck. Allocating funds specifically to certain categories decreases the mental load when thinking about money. Donating was also linked to increasing the sense of happiness. Dedicating certains amounts to having fun and treating yourself is an essential component of a healthy budget.

\*\*\*\*

One of the things you can also do is **aligning meal prep with your budget**. Preparing meals in advance prevents expensive takeout, reduces waste, and saves both time and money.

- Make a grocery list before shopping.
- Cook in batches and freeze extras.

- Track pantry staples so you don't buy duplicates.

---

**Microhabit Nudges:**

- ***Challenge yourself:*** *spend 10% less on groceries this week and put the savings in a separate jar, envelope, or account.*
- ***Automatic transfers:*** Move a set amount to your savings account the day you get paid.
- ***Check balances weekly:*** Set a reminder for Sunday. A glance at your accounts keeps surprises at bay.
- ***Review subscriptions:*** Cancel any you haven't used in 30 days.

---

This weekly financial commitment will increase your clarity and confidence. You don't have to track every dollar perfectly nor to eliminate all treats. You just need to know where you stand and make a few intentional choices.

Chapter 11

# Connection & Relationships

**W**eekends are not just for catching up on chores or planning the week ahead. They are also an opportunity to **reset your relationships**, reconnect with loved ones, and create meaningful moments that feed your soul. Our brains thrive on interaction, empathy, and shared experiences. Studies show that meaningful connections:

- lower stress levels and blood pressure.
- increase resilience during challenging times.
- improve mood and overall life satisfaction.

In fact, it has been found that spending an extra social time (at an average of 1.7 hours more during the weekend vs. during the weekdays) with friends and family is correlated with higher levels of happiness, even more so in males and full-time employees [17].

---

**Microhabit Nudge:** *Schedule one intentional conversation this weekend, even if it's just ten minutes of focused attention with someone you love.*

---

Owning your weekend is an opportunity to prioritize these connections. Small, deliberate interactions often matter more than long, distracted hours together. Some practical ways to strengthen bonds with those around you can include:

- **Shared meals:** Cook and eat together without screens.
- **Mini traditions:** Sunday morning walks, family game nights, or evening tea rituals.
- **Active listening:** Put away devices and ask meaningful questions.
- **Creative collaboration:** Art projects, home improvements, or DIY activities that involve everyone.

**Microhabit Nudge:** *Pick one interaction this weekend where you give your full attention. Notice how it changes the energy in the relationship.*

### Connection for Working Parents

If you're a working parent, the challenge is magnified. You're balancing deadlines, school runs, household responsibilities, and your own self-care. I know that first-hand. Finding space for connection can feel impossible, but it is **critical** for family harmony and your personal reset. Here are some recommendations:

## 1. Micro-Moments

Even ten minutes can have an impact. Use them intentionally. For example:

- A 5-minute check-in after breakfast with your child: "What's one thing that made you happy this week?"
- Sending a thoughtful text to your partner or child during the day.
- A short bedtime story, even on a busy evening.

## 2. Weekend Connection Blocks

Reserve 2–3 hour blocks specifically for family or social outings. Consistency is more important than length. Repeated, meaningful experiences create strong bonds with your loved ones. Consider:

- A Saturday park visit after resetting your space.
- A Sunday afternoon bike ride or picnic.
- Creative projects at home that involve everyone.

## 3. Delegate & Share Tasks

Working parents often feel they have to do everything. This weekend reset invites **shared responsibility**:

- Children can help with meal prep or tidying.
- Partners can alternate weekend chores.
- Outsource help or small tasks if possible.

## 4. Communication Rituals

Clarity in communication prevents conflict. Consider:

- Sunday morning family huddles to plan shared schedules.
- Mid-week check-ins (via video or phone if physical meetings cannot be accomplished) to maintain connection.
- Evening gratitude sharing: each person names one highlight from their day.

## 5. Self-Compassion

Finally, remember that connection doesn't have to be perfect. You may not have hours to spend together, and that is okay. **Presence matters more than perfection.** Do not be hard on yourself.

Check out the image below for a list of conversation starters that could help in getting ideas for what to talk about with your family.

Dedicating weekend time for connection isn't limited to family. Brief gestures with those outside your household can maintain social bonds and contribute to your long-term well-being. Other persons worthy of attention can include:

- **Friends:** Schedule a coffee, walk, or call.
- **Community:** Volunteer or attend a local event.
- **Mentors or colleagues:** Check in with someone who supports or inspires you.

Chapter 12

# Quiet & Creativity

Amid the busyness of the weekend (chores, errands, meal prep, social obligations) there is a space many of us overlook: the space for quiet and creativity. This is the part of the weekend that feeds your soul, sharpens your mind, and restores energy in ways even sleep cannot fully achieve. Quietness is more than the absence of noise; it is **being present with yourself**. It allows your brain to:

- process emotions and experiences.
- make connections between ideas.
- recharge from overstimulation.
- reconnect with your values and priorities.

Truly quiet moments can reset your nervous system. For those juggling multiple roles, this is not a luxury; it is a necessity.

Before we delve deeper into this chapter, I want to share with you the results of a study on the effects of weekend recovery [18]. The study concluded that individuals who engaged in psychological detachment from their workplace during the weekend were more recovered on Monday than those engaging in "mastery" activities, such as learning a new language or enrolling in a self-development class during the weekend. Another study, however, illustrated that participating in mastery activities during the weekend can help people increase their serenity and self-assurance by feeling more confident about their newly-gained skills [19]. This is important to note here to guide you towards choosing activities that cultivate a sense of relaxation rather than deeply engaging your mental psyche on Sunday.

## Creative Expression

Creativity is closely tied to quietness. It is not limited to artists or musicians; anyone can benefit. Quiet and creativity restore your energy, clarify your thinking, and allow your mind and spirit to uplift. Creative activities can look like:

- Writing in a journal or blog.
- Sketching, painting, or coloring.
- Photography.
- Gardening.
- Playing an instrument or experimenting with sound.
- Cooking new recipes or plating meals creatively.
- DIY projects or crafting.
- An old hobby you want to revive.

---

**Microhabit Nudge:** *Pick one creative activity this weekend and do it without measuring success.*

## Quiet & Creativity for Families

Finding this space as a working parent can be challenging. However, think about how even small pockets of time can be impactful for you and your children.

### 1. Micro-Moments

- **Early mornings:** 10–15 minutes of journaling before the household wakes up.
- **During meals:** Mindful eating (i.e., noticing textures, flavors, and gratitude).
- **Bedtime:** Reading or sketching.

### 2. Weekend Blocks

- **Saturday afternoon:** Combine family time with creativity. Do things like: baking together, making music, or building a small project.
- **Sunday evening:** Personal creative time after the household winds down.

These moments recharge both parent and family, modeling the value of creativity for children.

### 3. Combine Quiet and Connection

- Silent walks with a partner or child, noticing surroundings.
- Shared journaling: Everyone writes a short reflection, then reads aloud.
- Collaborative art projects: Painting a mural, scrapbooking, or decorating a space.

**Microhabit Nudge:** *Encourage children to pick their own creative project alongside yours. It reinforces autonomy and shared creativity.*

### Tips to Protect Quiet & Creative Time

1. **Set boundaries**: Let others know your creative or quiet time is non-negotiable.
2. **Minimize digital distractions**: Silence notifications, put devices away, or use a focus mode.
3. **Designate a space**: A corner of a room, a balcony, or a small desk can become your creativity zone.

4. **Combine sensory inputs**: Soft music, candles, or natural light can enhance focus and inspiration.
5. **Allow imperfection**: The goal is expression, not performance.

Before we end our journey in this book, ask yourself:

- What quiet moments felt most restorative this weekend?
- Which creative activities gave you joy or clarity?
- How can you integrate at least one of these into your weekday routine if time permits?

# Your 48-Hour Plan

By now, we have explored every corner of how to truly own your weekend: closing the week, refreshing your body and space, planning ahead, reconnecting with loved ones, and carving out time for soul, creativity, and focus. This chapter brings everything we have learned together in a **practical, repeatable blueprint**.

## Tips for Long-Term Success

- **Consistency beats intensity**: You don't need a perfect weekend every week.
- **Adapt to life's rhythms**: Some weekends may need flexibility and that's okay. Adjust the schedule to your life.
- **Celebrate small wins**: Completing even one key reset task counts as success. Recognize it and reward yourself.
- **Review monthly**: Every few weeks, glance back at your reflections to adjust priorities and microhabits.

The 48-hour reset plan flows naturally across Friday evening, Saturday, and Sunday. The recommended structure is:

## Friday Evening

Purpose: Signal the week's end and prepare your mind for rest.

- Close your week mentally
- Review accomplishments
- Brain dump lingering thoughts
- Journal reflections
- Reflect on one win of the week
- Turn off work notifications
- Create a small ritual to mark the week's end (e.g., lighting a candle, favorite tea, music)

## Saturday

Purpose: Restore energy, refresh your environment, and cultivate inner peace.

- Morning:
    - Coffee or tea ritual
    - Gentle movement or stretching
    - Mindful breakfast
    - Optional: journaling or short meditation
- Mid-morning:

- Quick tidy: make beds, load dishes, & declutter main areas
    - Laundry
    - Small organizing projects
    - Optional: a 15-minute focused cleaning sprint
- Afternoon:
    - Hydration, light exercise or walk, & nourishing meals
    - Optional outing: 2–3 hours with family, friends, or solo recharge
- Evening:
    - Optional: plan grocery lists, go on a trip to the store, then prep vegetables for meals

**Sunday**

Purpose: Plan, prepare, and create intentional space for the week.

- Morning:
    - Reflect on the past week
    - Prioritize Top 3 tasks for the week ahead
    - Schedule the week's essentials and intentions
- Mid-morning:
    - Organize groceries
    - Prepare simple, balanced meals for the week

- Prep at least one grab-and-go meal for Monday
- Afternoon:
  - Digital detox
  - Review bills and upcoming payments
  - Allocate spending for essentials and one intentional treat
- Evening:
  - Schedule quality time with family or friends
  - Micro-moments: check-ins with children, partner, or friends
  - Express gratitude or share reflections
  - Dedicate time for creative expression or silent reflection
  - Combine quiet and connection where possible (e.g., silent walks or collaborative art)
  - Designate & protect at least one personal creative block

---

**Microhabit Nudge:** *Keep this weekend structure visible (psst! See image below) in your planner, on your fridge, or as a note on your phone to guide your reset every week.*

## Further Microhabits

The beauty of this book lies in its integrated microhabits. Additional examples to those mentioned in the book include:

- Before bed, write down *one sentence* about something you're grateful for that day.
- Take five slow breaths before lying down in bed.
- Turn off bright overhead lights and switch to a soft lamp or candle 30 minutes before bed.
- Do *one* set of any bodyweight exercise (push-ups, squats, or planks) once a day.
- Replace one elevator or escalator trip per day with the stairs.

- Play one upbeat song you love and move/dance to it.
- Put your phone on airplane mode ten minutes before bed and read a physical page of anything instead.
- Give one genuine compliment to someone every day.
- Set a timer for three minutes, walk around (inside or outside), then return to work.
- Stand up for one minute during some (or every) commercial break or ad.
- Stand on one leg while brushing your teeth.
- Place a warm compress or heating pad on your shoulders for two minutes.
- Text one person: "Thinking of you today."
- Send one short voice message instead of a typed one.
- Keep fruit visible in a bowl. Eat one when craving a snack.
- Ask your child one specific question: "What made you laugh today?"
- Tie one habit to another (e.g., stretch after brushing teeth).

**Microhabit Nudge:** *Each weekend, choose one new microhabit to integrate.*

At the end of each weekend, take a few minutes to ask yourself:

- What helped me reset internally the most this weekend?
- Which microhabits felt easiest to implement?
- What could I adjust next week to make the 48-hour plan smoother?
- How did my energy, focus, and relationships feel after this experience?

# Conclusion

As you've explored through this book, owning your weekend starts with aligning four key elements: **mind, body, environment, and relationships.** Each chapter has shown that small, intentional steps (i.e., microhabits) create momentum that compounds week after week. Adopting this mindset will allow you to intentionally pause, reflect, and care for your life every weekend.

You will start to feel self love and care when you repeat and consistently apply the strategies outlined here *every weekend*. Mix and match the different activities suggested in this book. Over time, your mind will learn that Friday evenings are for closure, Saturdays are for refreshment and a sense of reward, and Sundays are for planning, reflection, and having fun! Even if you don't complete every step perfectly, **showing up consistently** is what builds lasting transformation.

## Resetting Beyond the Weekend

While the book focuses on Friday through Sunday, the principles covered herein can ripple through your week:

- Use microhabits during short breaks at work.
- Reflect and journal at the end of busy days.
- Carry small rituals, like mindful coffee breaks or gratitude notes, into weekdays.

Every reader's reset weekend will look different. Your space, responsibilities, relationships, and energy levels are unique. That's why this book provides a flexible weekend schedule blueprint.

- Adapt the schedule to fit your life.
- Choose microhabits that resonate with you.
- Experiment and iterate.

Additionally, having a refreshing weekend doesn't just benefit you. It impacts those around you: family and friends feel your presence more fully, colleagues notice your focus, and your community benefits from the energy you bring in. By caring for yourself intentionally, you create space to care for others more effectively.

**Microhabit Nudge:** *Consider sharing your weekend plan with someone close. Invite them to join you one weekend.*

---

Start small. Pick one aspect of the suggested schedule this weekend. Maybe it's Friday evening reflection, a 20-minute Saturday tidy-up, or a Sunday planning session. Experience it fully, notice the difference in your spirit, then build from there. **This book is not about perfection but about creating awareness and intentionality in your life.** Every Friday night lights off, every meal prepped, every micro-moment of connection is a step toward a more organized and fulfilling life.

# References

[1] Volpp, K. G. and Loewenstein, G., What is a habit? Diverse mechanisms that can produce sustained behavior change. *Organizational Behavior and Human Decision Processes*, *161*, 2020, 36-38, https://doi.org/10.1016/j.obhdp.2020.10.002.
[2] Burke, W. W., A Perspective on the Field of Organization Development and Change: The Zeigarnik Effect. *The Journal of Applied Behavioral Science*, *47*(2), 2010, 143-167. https://doi.org/10.1177/0021886310388161.
[3] Davidson L., Habits and other Anchors of Everyday Life That People with Psychiatric Disabilities May Not Take for Granted. *OTJR: Occupational Therapy Journal of Research.* 27(1), 2007, 60S-68S. https://doi.org/10.1177/15394492070270S108
[4] Sian Beilock, *How the Body Knows Its Mind: The Surprising Power of the Physical Environment to Influence How You Think and Feel.* New York, NY, USA: Atria Books, 2015.
[5] Ferrari, J. R. and Roster, C. A., Delaying Disposing: Examining the Relationship between Procrastination and Clutter across Generations. *Current Psychology*, *37*, 2018, 426–431. https://doi.org/10.1007/s12144-017-9679-4
[6] Swanson, H. L. and Ferrari, J. R., Older Adults and Clutter: Age Differences in Clutter Impact, Psychological Home, and Subjective Well-Being. *Behavioral Sciences*, *12*(5), 2022, 132. https://doi.org/10.3390/bs12050132
[7] Saxbe, D. E. and Repetti, R., No place like home: home tours correlate with daily patterns of mood and cortisol. *Personality and Social Psychology Bulletin*, *36*(1), 2010, 71-81. https://doi.org/10.1177/0146167209352864
[8] Elmagd, M. A., Benefits, need and importance of daily exercise. *International Journal of Physical Education, Sports and Health*, *3*(5), 2016, 22-27.
[9] Giorgio, A. D., Kuvačić, G., Milić, M., and Padulo, J., The Brain and Movement: How Physical Activity Affects the Brain. *Montenegrin Journal of Sports Science and Medicine*, *2*, 2018, 1-6. https://dx.doi.org/10.26773/mjssm.180910

[10] Benton, D. and Young, H. A., Do small differences in hydration status affect mood and mental performance? *Nutrition Reviews*, *73*(2), 2015, 83–96, https://doi.org/10.1093/nutrit/nuv045

[11] Minich, D., Colorful Foods for Health and Well-Being. *Journal of Integrative and Complementary Therapies*, *31*(4), 2025, 147-151, https://doi.org/10.1089/ict.2025.70710.dm

[12] Chumachenko, Y. S., et. al., Keeping weight off: Mindfulness-Based Stress Reduction alters amygdala functional connectivity during weight loss maintenance in a randomized control trial. *PLOS One*, 2021. https://doi.org/10.1371/journal.pone.0244847

[13] Dominguez, L. J., Veronese, N. and Barbagallo, M., The link between spirituality and longevity. *Aging Clinical and Experimental Research*, *36*(32), 2024. https://doi.org/10.1007/s40520-023-02684-5

[14] Lee, X. Q., Decision Fatigue Effect. In: Raz, M. and Pouryahya, P. (eds). *Decision Making in Emergency Medicine*, 2021, 103-110. Springer, Singapore. https://doi.org/10.1007/978-981-16-0143-9_17

[15] Uğur, N. G. and Çalışkan, K., Time for De-cluttering: Digital clutter scaling for individuals and enterprises. *Computers & Security*, *119*, 2022, 102751. https://doi.org/10.1016/j.cose.2022.102751.

[16] Chennai, T. N., Digital Hoarding: The Rising Environmental and Personal Costs of Information Overload. *Partners Universal Multidisciplinary Research Journal*, *1*(2), 2024, 51-67. https://doi.org/10.5281/zenodo.12802575

[17] Helliwell, J. F. and Wang, S., Weekends and Subjective Well-Being. *Social Indicators Research*, *116*, 2014, 389–407. https://doi.org/10.1007/s11205-013-0306-y

[18] Wyngaarden, G. V., ""Did you have a good weekend?" A week-level diary study examining the relationship between weekend recovery and weekday performance," M.C. thesis, Faculty of Commerce, University of Cape Town, 2021.

[19] Fritz, C., Sonnentag, S., Spector, P. E. and McInroe, J. A., The weekend matters: Relationships between stress recovery and affective experiences. *Journal of Organizational Behavior*, *31*(8), 2010, 1137-1162. https://doi.org/10.1002/job.672

# About the Author

Dr. Tila graduated from the University of Toronto in 2024 with a degree in Mechanical Engineering. She has a passion for science, arts, and home organization. Her new experience as a mom opened her eyes into how working parents can juggle many tasks at once. She also has lived in numerous countries and cities. Combined, these experiences inspired Dr. Tila to share tips and tricks with the world through books, handbooks, and planners & motivate intentional living.

If you reached this far, please consider leaving a review or star rating on the platform you bought the book from to help others make a decision.

www.ingramcontent.com/pod-product-compliance
Lightning Source LLC
Chambersburg PA
CBHW071724020426
42333CB00017B/2384